MORE
THAN
ENOUGH!

Kevin Mullens

FZM Publishing
2013

Copyright 2013
By Kevin Mullens

All Scriptures, unless indicated, are taken from the King James Version (KJV).

Scripture quotations marked NIV are taken from the New International Version.

Scripture quotations marked NLT are taken from the New Living Translation.

ISBN
978-0-9891997-2-8

Printed in the United States of America

Table of Content

Foreword

"I have known Kevin Mullens for almost a decade. God has deeply burdened his heart for those in need. In the network marketing industry, Kevin has built a reputation as a man who knows that reaching your goal is too important to leave to chance. Kevin has not only built financial success for himself, but has also helped many people accomplish financial success in a way they never imagined. If you want the maximum life with minimum strife, internalize Kevin's wisdom. Kevin is a master at planning, planting, nurturing and harvesting. I am so proud to call Kevin Mullens my friend."

- Paul Orberson
  Million Dollar a Month Earner in the Direct Selling Industry

"Minister K. Mullens has proven himself to be a great leader and speaker inside and outside the church! We met years ago, and we've been cool ever since! He's been there as a friend, confidant, etc. He is always willing to help in any way he can! Minister Mullens is someone you can call on and trust to be honest, truthful, upright, etc. He will keep your conversation confidential! I may not have heard everything, but I have never heard one bad thing about this great man of God!"

- Joey Williams
  6 time Grammy Award Winner with Blind Boys of Alabama

"I have worked closely with Kevin Mullens for three years now and have the highest regard for his integrity and his character. You can rely absolutely on anything that he says about himself, his business or his ministry."

- MJ Durkin
  Author of *"Double Your Contacts"* and the creator of Recommendation Selling™

"I immediately discerned that Kevin Mullens was a great leader when I was first introduced to him. His obsession for success is incredible. His focus and heart is to increase people to their fullest potential. He is anointed to lead... gifted for increase... persuaded to advance the Kingdom of God. He not only speaks as a leader, but he walks as one too. I believe that all those who invest their time in extracting the principles in his newest book, **<u>More Than Enough,</u>** will experience a life of great increase."

- Dr. Jerry A. Grillo, Jr.
  Bishop and Founder of the Favor Center Church in Hickory, NC

INTRODUCTION

"The thief cometh not, but for to steal, and to kill, and to destroy: I am come that they might have life, and that they might have it more abundantly." John 10:10

I have heard this scripture recited many times as I grew up in church and have been preaching the Gospel most of my life. This scripture was preached mostly in terms of *spiritual abundance* rather than *financial and physical authority*.

As many do in church, I used to say that we are inwardly wealthy. I never really placed this thought of John 10:10 to being a place we could walk in outwardly. The truth is that many do not know how to outwardly invoke this divine promise.

Because we see so many not walking in divine wealth or in divine prosperity, we are caused to live with unanswered questions. Why? Why does the Bible say we can have abundance but so few in churches have it? We deal with this lack, or loss, by becoming religious and spiritualizing our plight. We make having less "more holy" than having more. We have come to this conclusion that having money is evil. Money is meant for the few and not the many. We make up comforting statements; *"If God wanted us to have wealth He would have given it to us."*

Wealth isn't evil. Wealth isn't used just to promote the enemies agenda. Wealth is Godly. Wealth is God's divine plan, distorted by the enemy to keep those who could do well with it, not to have it.

In reality, money is a tool. Wealth is just a tool! In the hands of spirit filled believers wealth becomes dangerous to the enemy.

ARE YOU DEAD OR DANGEROUS?

What hell fears more than someone getting saved, is for someone who is saved to become wealthy! Attach money to anything and it amplifies what it touches. Money is simply that. It is a magnifier of what it's attached to. Give money to a drug addict and he becomes an addict of better drugs. Put money in the hands of a believer and they become influencers in their community. Money is merely a tool, and it always exposes what is in the heart. With wealth, we can:

- Give more
- Tithe more
- Build schools
- Fund our causes
- Eliminate debt

The Bible tells us that the rich would rule the poor because the borrower becomes a servant to the lender. The great thing is that we can choose which of these we want to be—the borrower or the lender. No one is going to follow the person who lives in a ditch. Sounds noble, but it is simply not true. Let me ask you a question. If you can't pay your bills, how can you really help anyone? If your neck is never above your own pile of debt, you are actually in no position to financially do anything for God. You can't help someone else until your own life has risen above even.

I meet people that tell me they are content living their life with no money. They are always lacking and needing someone to help them pay a bill or give them a loan. It's a lifestyle of bondage or volunteered slavery. I once asked a preacher to write down everything he could do with nothing. The answer of course was NOTHING!

We must begin to remove barriers that keep us from obtaining wealth based on theories or handed down dogma that holds no water. When you begin to discover how to unlock the secrets of abundance in your life, you will realize that making money was never hard to do, you just needed a blueprint to follow. What happens after you've reached even? You move into overflow. Now you're in a position to bless others. So in reality, we are blessed to be a blessing.

I have sat down to pen my thoughts about prosperity as it pertains to scripture so that you can walk free from the bondage of debt. It is time to end this crazy doctrine of poverty that has been lifted up as a badge of honor or holiness, when there is NO scripture to support it.

This book will cover a lot of scriptures that we know very well, and through simplicity of God's Word we will view things in a new light and truly recognize that poverty, or lack, is more a symptom of what's going on inside than out. If you change your words, you will change your destiny. Sounds silly I suppose, but the words we speak are either life or death. You are in control of the world you live in by the words you declare, for whatever you declare materializes and comes to pass.

Believers should talk differently than unbelievers. The wealthy always talk differently than those that live paycheck to paycheck. It's not enough to just read the scripture, but you must learn how to apply unwavering faith that the writer of the Word is able to fulfill His promises in your life.

It is my prayer that you will soon realize that having abundance or *more than enough* is just a reflection of the nature of Christ.

Chapter One

Reflecting Your True Identity

So many Christians bare the name "Christian" but often doubt that they are really made in His image or even designed for a greater purpose by the master architect Himself. Why do we allow our lives to be shaped by others opinions of ourselves? You get to choose what you become by the decisions you make, and no matter the inadequacies or failures that come your way, you must recognize your position as a son or daughter of God. This way, when you read scriptures that pertain to wealth or prosperity, you won't simply throw it aside as something meant for another time or even for others. You are a Joint-Heir in His kingdom, which means, what's His is yours. It's no different than having a joint checking account. Both have access to the funds. We are in covenant with a King who is the inexhaustible fountain of life, and His bank account is never in the negative. When you wake up the spiritual giant that lives inside, you will reach a place of maturity to see God's Word manifested in all areas of your life.

"Every man also to whom God hath given riches and wealth, and hath given him power to eat thereof, and to take his portion, and to rejoice in his labour; this is the gift of God." Ecclesiastes 5:19

I love the KJV on this scripture. It doesn't say, "it" is a gift of God. It says it is THE gift of God. Well, this alone could blow the doctrine of poverty out of the water. Yes, I know that Jesus is the real Gift and to accept Him is to accept all that He is. When Christ is established in your heart then all of His nature can be reflected in your life. You get to choose. As the Word says, *"I have set before you life and death, blessing and cursing: therefore choose life, that both thou and thy seed may live"* (Deuteronomy 30:15). Could you imagine anyone choosing poverty, death or a curse? To know God does not give you access to wealth; you must know His principles to create wealth. I meet many people that have read all the right books on influence, or mindset, but struggle internally on whether or not good things can happen to them. King David wrote that God takes pleasure in the prosperity of his servant. WOW!!! To think that God desires you to live well beneath your God given rights is ludicrous. He takes PLEASURE in you prospering, and not just in spiritual matters, but in all areas of your life. As He continues to give us increase, we continue to have many opportunities to brag on our Father. Challenge yourself to think differently so you can act differently, because as a man thinketh in his heart, SO IS HE. As Dr. Mike Murdock says, *"Today you should declare that I am the poorest I will ever be."*

It's a challenge to your faith to speak life, victory and abundance in the face of your circumstances. You see, your circumstances do not have to dictate your choices, but your choices do dictate your circumstances.

When you realize you are a magnet for whatever you focus on, you will realize that you are in control of the world you live in. Do not hide your talent in the ground, being fearful that you are inadequate to create value or succeed. Fear is premeditated failure and will paralyze you into never doing anything to advance the Kingdom of God.

"His lord answered and said unto him, Thou wicked and slothful servant, thou knewest that I reap where I sowed not, and gather where I have not strawed:Thou oughtest therefore to have put my money to the exchangers, and then at my coming I should have received mine own with usury. Take therefore the talent from him, and give it unto him which hath ten talents. For unto every one that hath shall be given, and he shall have abundance: but from him that hath not shall be taken away even that which he hath. And cast ye the unprofitable servant into outer darkness: there shall be weeping and gnashing of teeth." Matthew 25:26

We all know the story well, but notice how the Lord identified this servant that refused to create increase. He called him a wicked and slothful servant. What have we done in this journey with the talent God has given us? Do we rent this skill out to another man making him rich, building his dreams, or sending his kids to the best schools why we settle for a wage? Having a job is an honorable position to hold, but a JOB means you have a BOSS that dictates what you're worth per hour. That determines where you live, cars you drive, the vacations you can take and even the school your kids attend. Everything becomes predetermined by your hourly wage. There is nothing worse than having to beg for a few hours off to go watch your kid play ball or to attend revival.

The job is an amazing place to start because of the valuable lessons that can be obtained; but as you increase in knowledge and begin to awaken that entrepreneurial spirit within, you will desire more because you desire to DO MORE. We were created in His image, so we have the power to change our world and experience abundant blessings in our lives; but it starts with sowing in your own field and realizing, "If they can do it, then so can I."

On the contrary, the Lord speaks differently to the servants that created increase.

"His lord said unto him, Well done, thou good and faithful servant: thou hast been faithful over a few things, I will make thee ruler over many things: <u>enter thou into the joy of thy lord</u>." Matthew 25:21

Let us come together and put a stop to lack or poverty by accepting God's Word in our lives. May we start today being faithful over a few things, so we can be ruler over many things.

Start with the belief in ourselves and God's purpose for our lives being greater than what we have settled for. Solomon said, *"Wisdom is the principle thing"* (Proverbs 4:7). Hosea said, *"My people are destroyed for a lack of knowledge"* (Hosea 4:6). NOT EDUCATION. We have more education than we know what to do with. Education doesn't equal wealth. Wisdom on the other hand is entirely different. Solomon asked for wisdom, and wealth was the by-product. Proverbs tells us that wisdom is the principal thing and then it commands us to exalt her (wisdom). By doing so, she shall exalt thee and bring you to honor. That's shouting material!

I desire for all of us to hear those precious words from the master's lips, *"Enter into the joy of the Lord."* Today is truly the poorest you will ever be. I believe that from the time you finish this book and begin to journal your life from this point on, as you apply the Word under a newfound FAITH, you will see the Favor of God has always been on your life. Today, we declare a new destiny backed by the authority of God's Word. We recognize our position in His kingdom as we unlock these promises in our lives.

5 Kingdom Principles to Creating Wealth

Principle #1

The Power of Wealth Lies Within You

Law of Recognition:

Everything you need is not coming to you. It's not in your future waiting on you to arrive. It's not hidden in your day nor is it hidden in some secret place waiting on you to find a treasure map, or some genie in a jar. The power of wealth is hidden in the secret place of your own mind.

"Now unto him who is able to do exceedingly abundantly above all that we ask or think, according to the POWER that works in us." Ephesians 3:20

I once preached a message, "God never gives me what I ask for," suggesting of course that this scripture gives us insight into the nature of our Father. This passage is often quoted, but very seldom ever manifested. Now, it does not say He would give us exceedingly abundantly above all that we ask or think. It says He is ABLE TO. This means there is a role for you to play in order for God's Word to materialize. I love that God never gives me what I ask for.

This passage unveils a quality of Jesus that few ever experience. I realized that when I ask for something in prayer with my belief, His answer is typically Exceedingly, Abundantly and Above All that I could ask or think. Obviously our mindset plays a major role in experiencing these blessings. Before a word is ever a word, it's first a thought. The battle most lose is in the mind. Jesus stated that there first must be a renewing of the mind. You must take on the mind of Christ to become a born again Christian. In His mind, there are no limitations—the impossible is possible—mountains are moved.

Many books are written on the millionaire mindset. I believe the real millionaire mindset comes from the B-I-B-L-E. Solomon said, *"As a man thinketh in his heart, so is he"* (Proverbs 23:7). Wake up and realize that the One who is making these promises, lives within you. You will create a new destiny on earth when you apply faith to these words and truly believe them.

The last part of this scripture is the key to manifesting these sovereign principles in your own life, *"According to the POWER that works in us."* We read in Deuteronomy 8:18, ***"But thou shalt remember the LORD thy God: for it is he that giveth thee power to get wealth."***

There must be a connection between you and the spirit of God until your words become His words, and there are no limitations placed on your life anymore. Negative leaves and only positive enters. Whatever you believe is what you say and whatever you say determines who you are. We have been in control of our lives up to this point, so it's nobody's fault that we are where we are, but our own.

What is this POWER? ***"And, behold, I send the promise of my Father upon you: but tarry ye in the city of Jerusalem, until ye be endued with power from on high"*** (Luke 24:49).

He then tells us in Acts 1:8, ***"But ye shall receive power,*** *after that the Holy Ghost is come upon you: and ye shall be witnesses unto me both in Jerusalem, and in all Judaea, and in Samaria, and unto the uttermost part of the earth."*

To every Christian let's first go back and remember that the very word Christian means, to be Christ-Like. The Holy Ghost is the very life of Jesus living within you so that you can live on earth as a "minor" God; no not an object of worship, but as a son or daughter of God. **It's when you begin to declare your "I AM" consciousness.**

Moses asked the burning bush, who should I tell them has sent me? He replied, *"Tell them I am that I am has sent you"* (Exodus 3:14). Notice, when Moses confronted Pharaoh, he didn't say, "Let God's people go," but he said, "Let MY PEOPLE go." Moses began to recognize that he was representing God on earth, and he needed only to speak the Word. I am not suggesting that you are Moses, but the God that lived in Moses is still the SAME, yesterday, today and forever.

A story was once told about an orphanage found in a village in Vietnam. During the war, the teachers of this orphanage knew they had to get the kids to safety. One of the teachers leading this charge became paralyzed by fear of the circumstances and doubted she could lead these children through the mountains to a safe place. A young girl with a child's faith approached the teacher and said, "Just as Moses led the children of Israel through the Red Sea, I know you can lead us through the mountains to safety." The teacher replied, "I am not Moses," and the little girl with strong faith said, "You may not be Moses, but God is still God!"

You should declare, *"I am healed, I am redeemed, I am blessed and highly favored, I am saved by grace, I am wealthy and I am prosperous."*

It is this Power that molds and shapes a new world by the words that you speak, and knowing those words are backed by a supernatural POWER.

Some examples of "**MORE THAN ENOUGH**":

The Gospels give account of a story of Jesus feeding 5,000, besides women and children. We see this **MORE THAN ENOUGH** attribute on display here. Obviously Jesus, knowing all things, knew exactly how many mouths to feed; but it's as if He cannot help proving himself. The scripture tells us that the next morning the disciples picked up twelve baskets full of bread, once again identifying the abundant nature of Christ.

In another passage, we see this **MORE THAN ENOUGH** attribute of Christ in full effect again. We find the disciples out all night fishing and catching nothing. As they journey inland, they see a man on the bank named Jesus who instructs them to launch back out; but this time to drop their nets on the right side of the boat. We see a great example here of heeding a mentors instructions. Proverbs 13:18 says, *"Poverty and Shame shall be to him that refuseth INSTRUCTION."* You see the Word of God does not change you, but it is what you do with His Word that will change you. The disciples caught so much fish that they called for a nearby ship to come, and they filled two boats. Do you not think an all knowing God knew just how much fish would fill the disciple's boat? Of course He did, but He cannot help proving himself. If we follow these patterns, you can see God displaying himself in ABUNDANCE everywhere we look. Invoking these principles with Faith will bring this **MORE THAN ENOUGH** nature of God on the scene every time.

There is another scripture we often quote but never see manifested in our natural lives. Luke 6:38 declares, ***"Give, and it shall be given unto you; good measure, pressed down, and shaken together, and running over..."*** We have all given at different times. Why does it seem like some have favor and others don't? How can so many attend the same church, read the same Bible, have access to the same Savior, and yet the majority lives on barely enough to get by and are constantly fighting debt, while others seem to have figured out this abundant thing in all areas of their life. Our Father is not simply blessing some more than others because He likes one and doesn't like another.

Most Christians are missing the Wisdom to take God's Word and apply it properly. Creating wealth isn't doing certain things, but rather doing things in a certain way. We just read how He will give back to you pressed down, shaken together and running over. He being omnipotent knows how much your cup will hold, but once again, He cannot contain Himself from pouring out so much blessing that it runs over. It could almost appear wasteful, but it's not. It's the nature of a King who lacks nothing.

Principle # 2

Releasing the Power of the TITHE

In another portion of God's Word we read of a law that is absolutely key to activating God's economy.

"Will a man rob God? Yet ye have robbed me. But ye say, Wherein have we robbed thee? In tithes and offerings. Ye are cursed with a curse: for ye have robbed me, even this whole nation. Bring ye all the tithes into the storehouse, that there may be meat in mine house, and prove me now herewith, saith the LORD of hosts, if I will not open you the windows of heaven, and pour you out a blessing, that there shall not be room enough to receive it." Malachi 3:8-10

Tithing is a law, that if put into place, will create blessings regardless of your religion. Tithing correctly, which is ten percent from the first fruits and paying this to the right person (your pastor), plays an important role as well. Often when someone comes to me with a financial issue in their life and claims to be a believer, the first question I ask them is, *"Do you HONOR the Lord by paying tithes?"*

Stop thinking only ten percent belongs to Him. One

hundred percent belongs to Him, but He only requires ten percent. When you pay this properly, the remaining ninety percent becomes blessed. There is zero chance of you having God's FAVOR in your finances if you do not pay tithes. I would even suggest that if you are in covenant with someone who doesn't pay their tithes, that you break this covenant NOW!!! Anyone who will ROB GOD will ROB YOU. Do not gamble with God on this law. I would challenge you to start a journal today of everything that has supernaturally come your way in the realm of finances when tithing correctly. It is the only principle where you have a right to PROVE GOD; a respectful challenge that you have done what is required and in return He is obligated to bless you.

As you know, we are called the royal seed of Abraham, and Abraham lived under "grace" not the law. Yet, he was the first one to introduce "tithing" to the seed of Abraham. How often we miss the divine order in God's Word. It is this order that manifests His promises in our lives. **Abraham never staggered at the promise**. We need to follow Abraham's example so we can see the blessings of God in our families present and future.

Brother William Branham said, *"And to you people that don't believe in tithe paying, look at this. The Levitical priesthood paid tithes. And the Bible said that Levi paid tithes when he was in the loins of Abraham, and that was his great, great grandfather. And when Levi was in the loins of Abraham, when Abraham paid tithes to Melchizedek, the Bible reckoned Levi paying tithes. How ought you people to live? If your sins are visited to the children, what about your blessings?"* (FAITHFUL ABRAHAM title LA.CA 59-0415E)

Notice here that the seed (tithe) was sowed into good ground (Melchizedek). He paid tithes into a ministry that could provide INCREASE in his family's lives. We must recognize our role in generational blessings as it pertains to our families. If this seed of tithe is properly sowed with faith into the right ministry, then expect true abundance, wealth and prosperity in every area of your life, as it is written in the scripture.

I want to show you once again this **MORE THAN ENOUGH** nature of Jehovah. Here we find a promise that if you simply pay your tithes and believe the promise with unshakeable faith, God will pour you out a blessing that there will not be room enough to receive it. WOW!!! Now, ask yourself how many times you have paid your tithes and received a blessing so abundant in nature you didn't even have room enough to contain it? Most would say, "never." If you do not see this manifest in your life, does that make God a liar? Most people would answer "no." These principles can only be appropriated by FAITH in order to see these promises manifested.

Let's dig deeper to see if we are communicating these principles properly. The SECRET is EXPECTATION. I hear so many say, "I'm not expecting anything from the Lord." Why even plant seed if you do not expect it to bring forth a harvest? These laws of sowing and reaping are sovereign. If you have sown good seed in the right ground, it'll produce life. If you sow with great expectation you'll see heaven open up on your behalf and pour out a blessing for you that there won't be room enough to receive.

Our tithes do not merely bring a financial blessing, but verses 11-12 says, *"And I will rebuke the devourer for your sakes, and he shall not destroy the fruits of your ground; neither shall your vine cast her fruit before the time in the field, saith the LORD of hosts. And all nations shall call you blessed: for ye shall be a delightsome land, saith the LORD of hosts."*

How profound is God's love and favor toward us when we follow simple instruction. He desires to bless us abundantly, and then as a Father, protect us against our enemy. Do not remove this promise from your life and household by being disobedient. As much as we need Him to mightily bless us, we also need Him to put that hedge around us to preserve what He has given us that we might be a blessing to others. We are to be recognized by nations as a blessed group, not a group living in the land of not enough.

We find the Lord using David in the very beginning of Psalms instructing us on how to have true prosperity.

"Blessed is the man that walketh not in the counsel of the ungodly, nor standeth in the way of sinners, nor sitteth in the seat of the scornful. But his delight is in the law of the LORD; and in his law doth he meditate day and night. And he shall be like a tree planted by the rivers of water, that bringeth forth his fruit in his season; his leaf also shall not wither; and whatsoever he doeth shall prosper." Psalms 1:1-3

David wrote in Psalms 105 about mighty Jehovah bringing the children of Israel out of bondage with silver and gold, and not one was feeble among them. David was well aware of God's plan for the children of the LIVING GOD to be blessed. God's intent was to give them a land flowing with milk and honey. King David needed only to meditate on God's Word, and apply the Word to his life. Prosperity and success was simply a byproduct of doing such. Remember, it's not enough to just read the Word or say that you know Him. That alone is not enough to release the Favor of God. We need to know His principles, and once applied with the power of expectation and great faith, you will find blessings, favor, success and abundance so you may advance the Kingdom of God on this side of eternity and represent the **MORE THAN ENOUGH** nature of our Father.

Principle # 3

Words Unlock Your Prison or Create Your Prison

Your future is attached to your conversation. If you don't like where you are, change your conversation.

Brother William Branham was a modern day vindicated prophet who walked in a realm that few have ever walked. Over 200,000 visions and dreams and not one ever failed. A seventh grade education never limited his abilities, because he surrendered himself to a God that cannot FAIL. Yes, his supernatural gift and anointing gave him a sovereign gift so he could just speak the word and the God of heaven would come back it up. He constantly challenged the believers to operate in PERFECT FAITH. If we but recognized our place in HIM we could clearly identify that as sons and daughters of God we have authority to move mountains. Read this quote from a message preached in 1960.

"Now, man... I was going to choke it, but I'm going to say it. Man is omnipotent. You don't believe that, but he is. A man that's fully surrendered to God is omnipotent. Did not He say in Mark 11:22, "Whatsoever things you say and don't doubt in your heart, it'll come to pass. You can have what you've said?" What happens when two omnipotence meet? When

God and man come together through omnipotence, something's got to shake. Some... Whatsoever you'd say with that creative power of omnipotence of God, knowing that He's promised it, and He said it in His Word, it creates a power that goes out yonder and brings things to pass; things that is not, it makes them as though they are, because two omnipotence have met. There He stands. Oh, isn't He wonderful." The Patmos Vision, December 4, 1960 (tape #60-1204E)

Now, I am not suggesting that you are a vindicated prophet, but I am suggesting that we have a role to play as believers. Instead of accepting everything negative or impossible, you should start today by declaring whatever you desire. The spoken Word is a very powerful thing when spoken in FAITH.

What leads us to finding out how to declare the Word in such a way that we can see these promises materialize in our lives? The answer is of course, FAITH. It's speaking something with such belief, that your word doesn't go forth and come back void; but it begins to unveil a world that has always existed, but you didn't know how to access it. Saying the word is not enough. Anyone can remember words and recite them. It takes a genuine believer to push aside current circumstances and see that God desires to fill your life with abundance—in every aspect of your life—and He has given you POWER to see it happen.

In the book of Matthew, Jesus' authority was being questioned and here is the scripture that challenged their mindset, *"And all things, whatsoever you shall ask in prayer, believing, you shall receive"* (Matthew 21:22). When you really view this passage, it displays the POWER that God rendered unto the saints and once again shows us that God's intent was never for you to have nothing and live a life impacting no one. **Stop refusing to accept these**

promises as if they're fiction and cannot be applied to your life.

We know that it is impossible to please God without faith (Hebrews 11:6). This puts faith in a whole new light. It's the difference in being blessed or not. The apostle Paul said, *"Faith comes by hearing and hearing by the Word of God"* (Romans 10:17). Paul then explains that you cannot hear without a preacher and the preacher cannot preach unless he be sent (Romans 10:14-15). So we see that you need an anointed mentor to teach you what you do not know. A mentor is someone with a blueprint on how to get to where you've never been. Unto everyone is given a measure of faith, but it will take UNWAVERING FAITH to activate God's Word in your life in a supernatural way. This ultimately means you need a messenger. You need one to show you the way as Elisha had with Elijah, and in more recent times, as Napoleon Hill had with Andrew Carnegie and Tony Robbins had with Jim Rohn.

Find a mentor that can teach you how to make the right decisions and isn't afraid to correct you or challenge you so you may reach your full potential. A mentor is often a GPS or road map leading and guiding you to a place you have never been so at the appointed time, you will stand in front of those who God has placed in your care; leading them and empowering them so they may lead others.

It's important that you connect with the right people. Your friends are a prophecy of where you are going. If you can't change them, CHANGE THEM. Even Deuteronomy 22:10 says, *"You shall not plow with an ox and a donkey together."* God is definitely not a racist, but He has always been a separatist; constantly separating light from dark and the believer from the unbeliever. Ask God for divine connections and wisdom to recognize them as the Shunnamite women did with Elijah. When God wants to bless you, He sends a man. When Satan wants to curse you, he also sends a man. Be watchful and judge all things by the Word so you walk in FAVOR.

Scripture shows us in Genesis 39:5 the importance of recognizing the right people to honor and be in covenant with. *"The Lord blessed the Egyptian's house for Joseph's sake."*

The blessing of the Lord was ALL that he had. We must learn a valuable lesson from the Egyptian; he discerned where INCREASE and FAVOR was and by identifying this he was blessed mightily.

We read in Hebrews chapter four how the two and a half million that originally came out of bondage by the leadership of Moses never inherited the promise land because of their UNBELIEF.

Isn't it amazing that after seeing the hand of God deliver them in a supernatural way, that less than three days into their journey they started complaining? After forty years in the desert it came time to enter into the promise that God had already given them through prophecy, but out of two and a half million, only two people made it in. You see, no matter how hard Moses tried, the Israelites had come out of Egypt, but Egypt had never come out of them. So many believers today are just make believers. They have allowed the bondage of poverty to enslave their minds into believing that freedom, abundance, or prosperity by kingdom principles isn't made for them. Everything about Canaan represented prosperity. It was a land flowing with milk and honey and was rightfully theirs, but they feared the process of crossing Jordan, which represented death. They were unwilling to die out to their old thought patterns and recognize that they were born royalty.

The Bible tells us that Joshua and Caleb had a different sprit—one that never doubted the promises of God. Notice the ten spies made a confession of doubt as Joshua and Caleb made a positive confession.

"This book of the law shall not depart out of thy mouth; but thou shalt meditate therein day and night, that thou mayest observe to do according to all that is written therein: for then thou shalt make thy way prosperous, and then thou shalt have good success." Joshua 1:8

We have here in the first chapter of Joshua a guideline for being prosperous and successful. The first thing we recognize is the connection between the words we speak and success. It's very evident that true success is a direct result of keeping God's Word. He said, *"If you love me you'd keep my commandments."* Joshua, being mentored by Moses, saw this principle in effect first hand. He knew what position he held, and as a follower of Moses, he understood Kingdom principles and what his assignment was. Joshua led millions into the Promise Land. Those he led in were those that had been born in the desert and had never experienced slavery; therefore, their minds weren't polluted with serving in another man's kingdom.

You get to choose what side you want to be on. You can choose to accept life as it happens or you can go make life happen. The difference in having more than enough or having nothing is separated only by a razor's edge. The billionaires of the world are not coming down to teach us how to create wealth anytime soon. Most of us learn our business principles, or how to make money, from all the wrong people. Stop taking financial advice from broke people! Listen to how those around you communicate. **Change your words and you'll change your destiny**. The current infrastructure of our educational system is to teach you how to live based on a wage, but you can choose to own the field you sow in and live by profits.

The original Israelites that left Egypt couldn't rid their minds of the doctrine of the Egyptians. Every time it got tough they complained and desired life in slavery back in

Egypt, even though Psalms 105:37 says when God brought them out, *"He brought them out with silver and gold and none were feeble."* Even though they were endowed with all of these blessings, they could never change their mindset. It is how so many broke people win the lottery and in less than a year or two they are broke again. Your income always levels out to where your mindset and wisdom are.

It's kind of like the old story told of a farmer who finds an unusual egg out on his property and decides to bring it back to his farm to hatch. Once the bird is hatched, it immediately is out of place because it's an eagle that was born on a chicken farm. Even though its feathers are different and even its appetite is different, it spends most of its days just trying to fit in so it isn't teased as much. Maybe you have felt that way. Maybe you don't quite fit in and are not really sure why. It could be because you were always a Child of God, chosen from the beginning and ordained for a purpose; much like Abraham, you're just a stranger passing through while others seem to be content with whatever life gives them.

That mother eagle comes looking for that baby eagle one day and when it swooped down over that old farm and gave that eagle scream, there was something on the inside of that baby eagle that identified with that mother eagle. As David said, *"deep calleth unto deep"* (Psalm 42:7). You see that scream didn't bother or affect the chickens in any way because there was nothing inside of them to respond to the call. That day, the bird recognized it was born for freedom to soar the heavens, and today I pray that there's something in you that realizes you are a child of the most high King designed for abundance and to dominate the enemy.

Luke 12:32 declares, *"Fear not, little flock; for it is your Father's good pleasure to give you the kingdom."* Knowing that this is the desire of our heavenly Father, why then are so many believers struggling? Is it fear of the unknown, fear of failure, or just procrastination? I say rise up and take what's rightfully yours. Stop saying one day, someday, and almost. Recognize that you don't have to live in the land of not enough because you serve a God whose nature is **MORE THAN ENOUGH.**

Principal # 4

The Power of Reflection

YOU ARE NOT WHO YOU THINK YOU ARE, YOU ARE BIGGER THAN THAT!

"Beloved, I wish above all things that thou mayest prosper and be in health, even as thy soul prospereth." 3 John 1:2

You can't just throw this aside as only spiritual because this scripture has a compound meaning, both natural and spiritual. If you will "declare" this under a new light and recognize it's the Father's will that you prosper, you can unlock and experience MORE THAN ENOUGH. This scripture needs no interpretation; it plainly states that ABOVE ALL THINGS, He would that we would prosper and be in good health. Let's continue in our pursuit to recognize the things that can allow this to take place in our lives. The natural must reflect the spiritual.

On July 8th, 1959, Prophet William Branham said *"For Moses patterned the earthly tabernacle after what he had seen in heaven, a sanctuary of the Lord. Oh, I think that's so beautiful, to think that before God would let a church building be built, it had to be a pattern of His heavenly abode. Moses made all things after the pattern of the heavenly."*

We just established that it is the Father's good pleasure to give you the Kingdom, so let's break a few things down. In the book of Matthew we find the disciples asking about how to pray, and Jesus instructs them in chapter 6:9-10, *"After this manner therefore pray ye: Our Father which art in heaven, Hallowed be thy name. Thy kingdom come. Thy will be done in earth, as it is in heaven."*

This of course is a prayer we all learned as a child, but there is some profound revelation hidden within this prayer. Pay close attention to verse ten where He states, *"Thy kingdom come, Thy will be done in earth, as it is in heaven."* He declares His kingdom come, so where does the scripture tell us the kingdom of God is? Luke 17:21 tells us that the Kingdom of God is WITHIN YOU. Now that does not remove the fact that there is a literal Kingdom, but when you have accepted Christ, He then takes up His throne within your heart, making Him Lord of your life. Wherever the King is dwelling is also His kingdom. His very blood is coursing through your veins, and as a redeemed child of God, you gain access into the supernatural, which is what creates miracles.

Notice it then says, *"Thy will be done **in earth**, as it is **in heaven.**"* What exactly did God create Adam from? EARTH. You see, since that time, God has chosen the instrument of man to manifest Himself through. I really love the part, *"as it is in heaven."* So if the earthly is to reflect the heavenly, we must peek into heaven and see what is there. No crying, no sickness, no sin, no death, and definitely no POVERTY. The streets there are paved with gold. In 1 Kings 6:22 we see that the ENTIRE TEMPLE was overlaid with GOLD. Solomon understood wealth principles, through the wisdom of God, that his revenue source in building the temple had no limitations.

God desires for you to truly prosper as your soul prospers, and His will is to be done in earthen tabernacles where the Kingdom of God is, if the King is in your heart. His words and your words become one. You can say AMEN to every word spoken, and with a bulldog like faith, watch it go forth with boldness and materialize the things that you have spoken. The world titles it the "Laws of Attraction", but you cannot deny that the nature of God attracts His entire Word into your life. So stop asking yourself, *"Does the Lord want me to prosper?"* We find scripture piled on top of scripture conveying how generous God is toward the saints and His desire that you prosper. Here we find King David telling us:

"Let them shout for joy, and be glad, that favor my righteous cause: yea, let them say continually, Let the LORD be magnified, who has pleasure in the prosperity of his servant." Psalms 35:237

This doesn't need any interpretation. I hear people constantly saying, *"Whatever His will is"* or *"If it's His will."* This statement really gets me going and is such a cop out. His WILL is that none should perish, but many refuse to accept eternal life. It becomes a cop out to just tolerate whatever happens as if you have no control. In another portion of the Word we find an account of a rich young ruler and the story is often used to shed negative light on having money.

"It is easier for a camel to go through the eye of a needle, than for a rich man to enter into the kingdom of God. And they were astonished out of measure, saying among themselves, Who then can be saved? And Jesus looking upon them saith, With men it is impossible, but not with God: for with God all things are possible. Then Peter began to say unto him, Lo, we have left all, and have followed thee. And Jesus answered and said, Verily I say unto you,

There is no man that hath left house, or brethren, or sisters, or father, or mother, or wife, or children, or lands, for my sake, and the gospel's, But he shall receive an hundredfold now in this time." Mark 10: 25-30

Let's look at this event in detail. Jesus is not suggesting that having money is wrong. He spent more time talking about money in His time on earth than healing. We see a story being told that involved following an instruction by the Giver of Life. The young ruler admitted he had kept all the commandments but because he couldn't understand God's principles, he could not sow seed for harvest by giving all he had. The disciples overheard Jesus talking about how hard it would be for a rich man to enter heaven and they asked, **"WHO THEN CAN BE SAVED?"** You need to ask yourself, *"What would make Peter and the disciples standing there ask such a question?"*

Most living in poverty are not disgruntled if something happens to a rich man. You need to realize that Peter and other disciples were business men themselves. To even ask a question like this would suggest that standing there were men of wealth. Why would Peter be concerned about a rich man's possibilities of making it into heaven unless he himself had wealth? Jesus then says to them, *"It's impossible with man but with God all things are possible."* Then he turns to Peter and says, everything you give up for my sake I'll give back to you one hundredfold. WOW, **a one hundredfold blessing**! Then He tells him you will receive this blessing, **IN THIS TIME.**

His WILL can also be found in an often-recited scripture, *"For I know the plans I have for you," declares the LORD, "plans to prosper you and not to harm you, plans to give you hope and a future."* Jeremiah 29:11 NIV

Most of us have spent our entire lives learning how to make money, or even process money, from those who are broke or got a degree hoping it would automatically transfer into wealth. Hard work isn't the answer because we know a whole lot of hard working broke people, and a college degree—although important—isn't it either because you probably know many with multiple degrees who are broke as well.

It's been said that knowledge is power and ignorance is bliss. There is no way these two can co-exist. Ignorance is broke, not bliss, and it can be expensive as well. The Bible tells us that God's people are destroyed for a lack of knowledge. Knowledge is wisdom and you just can't learn that in a book. Wisdom comes from a mentor that has a blueprint on getting where you have never been before, and it operates in conjunction with faith. Solomon didn't ask God for education, he asked for wisdom and the byproduct of wisdom in the life of Solomon became wealth. We often say that to keep doing the same things over and over expecting a different result is the definition of insanity. WAKE UP!

How about we finally stop saying what we are going to do, and actually realize that we must start swimming upstream against the ideas, that for such a long time have created what some would call generational curses. During times of slavery it was against the law to teach a slave how to read, because if you educate a man, you liberate the man. On some levels we need to unlearn the ways we have been taught to make money and relearn this process so we can work smarter, not harder.

The billionaires of the world aren't just lucky. Luck has a way of happening to those that are well prepared and consistently active in areas that are productive. Here's what LUCK really is…

- Laboring
- Under
- Correct
- Knowledge

They have taken simple principles and applied them in the market place, and instead of simply trading time for money—earning a wage—they decided to create profits. In other words, if you sow in another man's field, come harvest time, you receive a wage and he gets the harvest. You need to own the field you are sowing in and take charge of your financial future. These kingdom principles can be applied by anyone, but we who are strong in Faith should recognize our position in God's kingdom and declare a new destiny as it relates to lack versus prospering.

You can be born again until you feel like you are ready for the rapture, but if you are making ten dollars an hour, you are still going to be making ten dollars an hour. Find a problem and solve it; see things differently. Instead of saying, I work for money, you could decide to make money work for you. Instead of saying whatever happens will happen, decide to think outside of the box and make something happen. We have been in control of our financial destiny all our lives and the place where we have arrived at today should not be a surprise. Be ye not conformed to this world; if you are following the majority you will fail. Jesus even said, "COME OUT," which means separate. If it were easy to be successful then everyone would be.

As a man thinketh in his heart, so is he. You do not have to live like the ninety-five percent of people who are barely getting by if you do not want to. You can decide today to take control and challenge yourself, stretch yourself and write the remaining chapters of your life in a different way. Will it be easy? NO! God never promised us a flower bed of ease. We go to work every single day building someone else's dream and sending their kids to the best schools while we sit by accepting whatever it is that they'll give us per hour; which dictates where we live, the cars we drive, where our kids go to school, where we vacation and for how long. Choose life abundant today in all areas of your life.

Principal # 5

Enlarge your thinking! Think BIG

The authority of Jabez prayer:

So often we quote the prayer of Jabez, "O that thou wilt bless me and enlarge my coast," without recognizing that if God is going to grant you favor and enlarge your territory there must be a battle. Can you imagine Abraham receiving the promise that 'wherever the soles of his feet trod', that it represented ownership and him staying in his living room? Abraham had to get out and do something about it. These promises are sovereign and God is not a man that He should lie. We know He did not speak them to go forth and come back void. We know what the Word says and now we must advance in our daily walk by putting these principles to work.

Poverty is a choice, and definitely not a badge of honor or a form of being more holy. When you are in lack, you have very limited choices. Little to no freedom, and rarely able to give the way you'd probably like. We know it's more blessed to give. The Bible tells us that when you give, it shall be given back to you, pressed down, shaken together and running over; once again establishing the, **MORE**

THAN ENOUGH nature of Christ. I am sure He knows just how much your cup can hold, but He just cannot help proving himself. Luke 3:11 says, *"He that hath two coats, let him impart to him that hath none; and he that hath meat, let him do likewise."* I've often said this scripture is a prime example of *lack* versus *abundance*. There's no way you can give someone a coat unless you have one. Material goods are not the subject matter here, but rather having enough for you and someone else that is in need. We know the love of money is evil and that lavish living can become destructive, but this is where the confusion sets in. Solomon said, *"money answers all things."* It's been said having money won't make you happy, but having no money surely won't make you happy.

At some point we must recognize that God's Word doesn't advocate poverty. I live near a city that was recently recognized as the eighth most dangerous city to live in by *Forbes* magazine. The cause mentioned in this article was low income and large pockets of poverty. It naturally attracts those who are up to no good. It's not a broad statement that poor people are bad people, but across the board you can typically identify this location in any town. It becomes a resting place for everything opposite of good. Having nothing makes you codependent on others, the government, or whoever will give you a handout.

Satan would love for you to continue living well beneath your God given rights, but you have a choice to take God at His Word and acknowledge that His desire for you is that above all things, you would prosper as your soul prospers.

The last part of the Jabez prayer is my favorite, **"And God granted him that which he requested."** The level of expectation has everything to do with prayer being answered. Matthew 21:22 says, *"ALL things, whatsoever you shall ask in prayer, BELIEVING, ye shall receive."* Now you either believe this scripture or you don't. God's Word holds no effect on your life if you have NO EXPECTATION. God desires to grant your request and answer your prayers as well. It is time we elevate our Faith so when we speak God's Word we expect it to materialize. Learn to be specific; so many pray vague prayers. If you need a financial blessing then specify how much you need, if you need a healing then specify what it is you exactly need. You must train your mind to hold an image of whatever it is you need or desire so your focus isn't shaken regardless of the circumstances. Even Job said that the thing he feared came upon him, so we must guard our thoughts and remain unmovable in our faith that what we have asked of God that He is bringing to pass.

As we continue to read and study God's Word my challenge for you is to stop looking at the Word as if it is a history book. The Word of God is as fresh today as it ever was. He's still the same yesterday, today, and forever. Your Faith toward the Word will determine what you get. Stop watching others transition into a different season in their lives as they see the blessings and favor of God happening in a profound way, as you remain complacent.

The scripture tells us that the Israelites were conquered by the Babylonians and Assyrians. They were captured, chained, and hauled off like animals to another country to become their slaves. After many years in captivity, they returned to their land; but the Israelites were a people with a broken spirit and had long forgotten what God had promised them. They were defeated and living life with a defeated mentality.

Success and failure all starts in the mind. They felt small. They were thinking small. They were in survival mode and playing it safe. God told them, "Enlarge your territories." He said, *"Enlarge the place of your tent, stretch your tent curtains wide, do not hold back; lengthen your cords, strengthen your stakes. For you will spread out to the right and to the left..."* (Isaiah 54:2-3).

The Israelites were a conquered people with a conquered spirit. Yet God says, *"It's time to conquer, it's time to dominate."* You should DECLARE, *"I AM not conquered, I AM an overcomer."*

God wanted them to make a switch from small thinking to big thinking. Believers, you may be like the Israelites. Perhaps you've been defeated by your problems and you think that the obstacles are just too big. Recently, you've been hammered by trials and haunted by your failures. You have a defeated spirit and are in need of revival. You see yourself as a small person and may have even stopped believing in your dreams. You've been thinking small in your bank account, or in your business, or in your family life, or in your ministry. God is challenging you even now, *"Don't think small."* Don't think survival. Instead, think BIG. Think growth. Think expansion and enlarge your territory. The mind of God is within you, so expect miracles to happen and believe the impossible is possible. The only limitations that ever truly exist are the ones you place on yourself. Never doubt again—whatsoever things God has promised, He can also keep. Get rid of all negative thoughts that would act contrary to a right positive mindset, and with much discipline, you will find yourself walking in true increase, overflow and favor. Wrong thoughts can create a season of discord and misery, where right positive thoughts backed by faith and expectation will create a season of abundance.

Closing Thoughts:

"Praise the LORD, How joyful are those who fear the LORD and delight in obeying his commands. Their children will be successful everywhere; an entire generation of godly people will be blessed. They themselves will be wealthy, and their good deeds will last forever. Light shines in the darkness for the godly. They are generous, compassionate, and righteous. Good comes to those who lend money generously and conduct their business fairly. Such people will not be overcome by evil.

Those who are righteous will be long remembered. They do not fear bad news; they confidently trust the LORD to care for them. They are confident and fearless and can face their foes triumphantly. They share freely and give generously to those in need. Their good deeds will be remembered forever. They will have influence and honor. The wicked will see this and be infuriated. They will grind their teeth in anger; they will slink away, their hopes thwarted." Psalms 112 (NLT)

I do not understand the depth of this chapter and all it entails, but the simplicity of this chapter resonates with me in a powerful way. Those that fear the Lord and obey His Word have a promise that their children will be successful everywhere. **THEY WILL BE WEALTHY.** Notice the prophetic boldness in the way God speaks about His children being blessed. They do not fear bad news; they are confident and fearless. We know that God has not given us the spirit of fear, yet so many of us live our lives in worry, stress, doubt and fearful of everything from failure to the unknown. When you recognize that you have already overcome because Jesus has overcome, you can then walk boldly in the promises of God. The story of Job tells us that the thing he feared most came upon him. This is why we must not tolerate negativity in our lives or it will consume our thoughts. If God be for us, then who can be against us? From this day forward you must cut ties with fear and recognize that NO weapon formed against us shall prosper. We have been well equipped to confront every obstacle, adversity or crisis and recognize that our enemy reveals our reward and represents a chance to be promoted.

Ralph Waldo Emerson said, *"The wise man in the storm prays to God, not for safety from danger, but deliverance from FEAR."*

When we embrace God's sovereign promises about us in HIS WORD concerning wealth, the windows of heaven will be open to us that they may flow through us.

Money is currency. It is meant to be transferred and used. Notice that the wicked are infuriated when they see the believer giving generously to those in need. We are commissioned all through the scripture to take care of the widow and the helpless. When your nature reflects that of your Father, you cannot help yourself. You are compelled to give. As we give with a cheerful heart, we are reminded that when you give, it is given back to you, pressed down, shaken together and running over. You just cannot out give God.

"He answereth and saith unto them, He that hath two coats, let him impart to him that hath none; and he that hath meat, let him do likewise." Luke 3:11

This is a great example of why we need to have abundance. If you do not have two coats then you cannot give one away. The enemy cannot stand to see you have honor and influence. It is a recipe for success in every area of your life.

David writes of a man whose house is in order. He fears the Lord. His life is established in God's Word so he has an anchor that is unmovable. Wealth and riches are in his house. WOW! We later see that this man knows what to do with the revenue God has blessed him with. He gives to the poor as Solomon said in Proverbs 28:27, *"He that giveth unto the poor shall not lack: but he that hideth his eyes shall have many a curse."*

We are well aware that we cannot out give God. You must step up and recognize wealth and riches, or prosperity, is just a part of God's desire in your life. Mainly so you can continue to advance God's kingdom on this side of eternity, enjoy life without the misery of living paycheck to paycheck or never having enough to be a blessing to your family— much less someone else's. This doesn't mean if you have nothing you aren't saved, no more than being rich means you can't enter heaven. Money just exposes what is in your heart. If you won't pay your tithes making one hundred dollars a week, you wouldn't pay your tithes if you were making one million dollars a week. It's just a tool. You just need to know that you can choose which one of these lives you choose to live.

Napoleon Hill studied billionaires for twenty-nine years. The simplest pattern he found among these very powerful and wealthy men was this thought, *"What the mind of man can conceive and believe, it can achieve."* This simple law is achievable by anyone. The believer has an advantage on everyone else because we have the Giver of Life living within us. When you unleash this power through unwavering faith in God's Word, you'll begin to see that obtaining what you thought was impossible or out of reach, was right before you all along just waiting on you.

"I call heaven and earth to record this day against you, that I have set before you life and death, blessing and cursing: therefore choose life, that both thou and thy seed may live..." Deuteronomy 30:19

This is so simple, **CHOOSE LIFE**. He chooses that you have life and have it abundant. If your heavenly Father chooses that for you, then you should make the right choice today.

King David had so many rich and in-depth writings on life. From heartaches to being a king with unlimited power, we are constantly reminded by David that in all things, give God glory and no accomplishment is worthwhile if we have eliminated Him from the picture. David knew what it was like to confront giants so that others might be free. David saw firsthand the penalty of breaking God's laws, and yet was a great witness of God's sovereign GRACE. I'm drawn to Psalms chapter 112 because it correlates with the theme of this book.

As you look for new endeavors to succeed in, so that you may walk in INCREASE, I want you to take this wisdom and apply it with faith and focus. I would like to suggest that you look at the potential of whatever it is that you put your hands to, and recognize its potential return on the principles you are applying.

You can apply these principles in the work place, but sometimes you still can only climb so high or earn so much because the JOB is limited to what you can make. You need to find something that will create cash flow and not just earning based on your time. We call this leverage. You will either create leverage, or you will be leveraged.

You can also create profits by selling a piece of real estate or even a car, but even this requires you to continue doing it in order to continue to earn money. At some point, you need to create in your life residual income. This is the ability to get paid over and over again for something you did one time. An insurance agent can write you a policy one time, but every month you pay the policy, the agent will receive royalties from it. In the world of wealth creation we call this cash flow. Figure out a way to earn recurring revenue based on something you did one time in a big time way. Be an entrepreneur. Entrepreneur is a God Word; it's a person with an idea. Before God ever spoke a word, it was first a thought. You must decide what you want, then find a vehicle that can get you where you intend on being.

Many billionaires—for instance—support direct sales because a regular person, from an ordinary background, with limited funds, can get involved and create leverage in today's market place; allowing them to generate an income that employment or traditional business just cannot compete with. Today's world has become very small through the internet. To think you can live where you live and generate income globally, is crazy, but none-the-less true. You see, no matter how bad we think the economy is, the truth is, that money didn't go anywhere; it just moved. Wherever money has moved to, is where you need to be.

I have always said, *"We know where money AIN'T."* In other words, we know where you cannot produce residual income or wealth. Identify something that can give you leverage so you are not co-dependent on only your efforts. Then through focus and alignment, be unusually determined to succeed. Make no excuses; accept no excuses. Your habits will change and your success will be hidden in your daily routine. Greatness is within you waiting to be manifested. It could be said that you already are what you will become; there is a giant waiting to be awakened. Speak those things that are not as though they are, and declare what it is you want, and then watch that thing come to pass.

Find something that will allow you to pour yourself into others. It is truly more blessed to give. The Apostle Paul said it best in 1 Corinthians 10:24, *"Let no man seek his own, but every man another's wealth."*

This is a key principle in obtaining wealth. If we could get caught up in seeking wealth for others then wealth, by default, materializes in our own lives. You can call this paying it forward or people helping people, but at its core it's a biblical principle that simply works. The problem is that it is a cut throat world in the work place, or most places of employment where everyone's intentions are typically to win at all cost no matter what.

Find something you can impart and empower others. Be sincere in wanting to help them succeed and you will wake up with a reward beyond explanation. You will either spend your days working for money or learn to make your money work for you.

Learn to reflect this MORE THAN ENOUGH nature of Christ in every area of your life, so you can be like Joseph was to his brethren in a time of famine. He alone became their supplier. Many are depending on us to step up and accept our calling because they are weak and need us to survive. I pray that you will rise up in your family, church, and community and be someone that proves anyone can do whatever they set their mind to do. Your story will inspire others to break the generational curse in their family against all odds and believe that ALL that God has written is obtainable by them as well.

Embrace the hard times—they build character. Never quit on your goals and dreams, no matter how many times you fail. Paul said, *"Be not weary in well doing, for in due season you shall reap if you faint not"* (Galatians 6:9).

Warfare is only Satan recognizing your future, so get some bulldog like faith, apply God's Word daily and watch prosperity unleash in your life like you have never seen before—Kingdom Prosperity.

About The Author

I grew up in a home with Holy Ghost filled parents that were prayer warriors. I lived in a small town in the panhandle of Florida along the Forgotten Coast. Although we never had wealth or abundance in material things, we more than made up for it with an abundance of love and creative imagination.

My mom and dad never held me back from dreaming and encouraged me to be all I could be, especially in the Lord. I would like to take this moment and apologize to my parents and my loving sister for the headaches and trouble I caused in my youth. I was a strong-willed son that often rebelled, but my heart was always tender towards the Lord. I was quick to repent and make things right.

My entrepreneur spirit comes from my dad and from my grandfather, O.P. Mullens, who was an apostolic preacher with a business mindset. He was always plotting and creating ways to obtain positive cash flow. He was fearless and was never afraid to take God at His Word. He believed that we had the power to obtain wealth as it is written in the Word.

I have always marched to a different beat than most and have dreamed BIG my entire life. There has always been this desire burning inside of me to lead and empower others; which I expressed at an early age by quitting school to preach the gospel.

My dad taught me to be my own boss and never serve in another man's field. My parents taught me the value of tithing, the art of giving and receiving on a daily basis, and how to be tough and not give up. I had the right mindset just not the right vehicle. I understood the necessity of having a true born again experience as well, so that Godly success might be obtained; giving God glory in all we do.

When I was 18 years-old, my life changed forever when I met a true angel on earth—my wife to be. My dreams and many plans of success have come at her expense. I have failed her and my wonderful boys often and definitely feel undeserving of them. In the midst of any chaos I caused, they always believed in me and my ability to help others.

I have always believed a man can conquer the world if he believes in himself, his Savior and has a spouse that believes and supports him. In any form of ministry, the family can often be neglected as you serve others. My source of life outside of Christ is my family. Today, we have the financial ability to be a blessing to many people in many different ways.

Failure has allowed me to succeed. My faith hasn't wavered regardless of obstacles I've faced; I have always been willing to try after failure and fight in the face of adversity. I have always believed that God will provide a way where there seems to be no way; if I ONLY **BELIEVE**.

I am honored to impart to you some wisdom I have received from many anointed mentors such as Pastor Luke Gibson, Dr. Jerry Grillo, Jr, Paul Orberson and many others that have impacted me in a profound way.

I pray your heart will be open to receive my message as it pertains to God's Word. *"For if two of you shall agree on earth as touching anything that they shall ask, it shall be done for them of my Father which is in heaven"* (Matthew 18:19). What would happen if we collectively pursued ending the poverty mindset and spirit of lack in one mind and one accord?

We all know we must do something different to get something different, so start today! The start is always the hardest in any endeavor worthwhile. You have the mind that was in Christ in you; dare to believe in the impossible being possible. Luke 1:37 says, *"With God NOTHING shall be impossible,"* so you must take God's Word and apply it with

UNWAVERING FAITH in all areas of your life, and watch favor and increase show up like never before.

Kevin Mullens